REFLECTIONS

FOR

LENT 2014

Church House Publishing
Church House
Great Smith Street
London SW1P 3AZ

ISBN 978 0 7151 4367 4

Published 2013 by Church House Publishing
Copyright © The Archbishops' Council 2013

The opinions expressed in this book are those of the
authors and do not necessarily reflect the official policy of
the General Synod or The Archbishops' Council of the
Church of England.

Designed and typeset by Hugh Hillyard-Parker
Printed and bound by CPI Group (UK) Ltd, Croydon, CR0 4YY

What do you think of *Reflections for Daily Prayer*?

We'd love to hear from you – simply email us at

publishing@churchofengland.org

or write to us at

Church House Publishing, Church House,
Great Smith Street, London SW1P 3AZ.

Visit **www.dailyprayer.org.uk** for more
information on the *Reflections* series, ordering
and subscriptions.

REFLECTIONS
FOR
LENT

5 March – 19 April 2014

IAN ADAMS
CHRISTOPHER COCKSWORTH
JOHN PRITCHARD
ANGELA TILBY

with an introduction by SAMUEL WELLS

Contents

About the authors

Ian Adams is a poet, writer and artist. He is the creator of the daily Morning Bell, author of *Cave Refectory Road: monastic rhythms for contemporary living* and *Running Over Rocks: spiritual practices to transform tough times*. Ian is an Anglican priest, director of StillPoint, and co-founder of Beloved Life. For more information visit: www.about.me/ianadams

Christopher Cocksworth is the Bishop of Coventry. He read Theology at the University of Manchester. After teaching in secondary education, he trained for ordination and pursued doctoral studies, serving in parochial and chaplaincy ministry and in theological education, latterly as Principal of Ridley Hall, Cambridge. Christopher is married to Charlotte and they have five children.

Stephen Cottrell is the Bishop of Chelmsford. Before this he was Bishop of Reading and has worked in parishes in London, Chichester, and Huddersfield and as Pastor of Peterborough Cathedral. He is a well-known writer and speaker on evangelism, spirituality and catechesis. His best-selling *How to Pray* (CHP) and *How to Live* (CHP) have recently been reissued.

John Pritchard is the Bishop of Oxford. Prior to that he has been Bishop of Jarrow, Archdeacon of Canterbury and Warden of Cranmer Hall, Durham. His only ambition was to be a vicar, which he was in Taunton for eight happy years. He enjoys armchair sport, walking, reading, music, theatre and recovering.

Angela Tilby is a Canon of Christ Church, Oxford and is Continuing Ministerial Development Adviser for the Diocese of Oxford. Prior to that she has been Vice-Principal of Westcott House, Cambridge and a senior producer at the BBC, where she made several acclaimed television programmes and series.

Samuel Wells is Vicar of St Martin in the Fields, London, and Visiting Professor of Christian Ethics at King's College, London. He is the author of a number of acclaimed books; his most recent titles are *What Anglicans Believe, Crafting Prayers for Public Worship* and *Learning to Dream Again*. He was formerly Dean of the Chapel and Research Professor of Christian Ethics at Duke University, North Carolina.

About *Reflections for Lent*

Based on the *Common Worship Lectionary* readings for Morning Prayer, these daily reflections are designed to refresh and inspire times of personal prayer. The aim is to provide rich, contemporary and engaging insights into Scripture.

Each page lists the lectionary readings for the day, with the main psalms for that day highlighted in **bold**. The Collect of the day – either the *Common Worship* collect or the shorter additional collect – is also included.

For those using this book in conjunction with a service of Morning Prayer, the following conventions apply: a psalm printed in parentheses is omitted if it has been used as the opening canticle at that office; a psalm marked with an asterisk may be shortened if desired.

A short reflection is provided on either the Old or New Testament reading. Popular writers, experienced ministers, biblical scholars and theologians will be contributing to this series. They all bring their own emphases, enthusiasms and approaches to biblical interpretation to bear.

Regular users of Morning Prayer and *Time to Pray* (from *Common Worship: Daily Prayer*) and anyone who follows the lectionary for their regular Bible reading will benefit from the rich variety of traditions represented in these stimulating and accessible pieces.

The book also includes both a simple form of Common Worship: Morning Prayer (see pp. 48–49) and a short form of Night Prayer – also known as Compline – (see pp. 52–55), particularly for the benefit of those readers who are new to the habit of the Daily Office or for any reader while travelling.

Making a habit of Lent

It's often said that life is about choices. But a life based on perpetual choice would be a nightmare. To avoid the tyranny of having to make perpetual choices, we develop habits. The point about habits is to develop good ones. That's what Lent is about. Here are the six most important ones.

- **Habit number one: look inside your heart.**

  Examine yourself. Find inside yourself some things that shouldn't be there. If they're hard to extract, get some help. Name them by sitting or kneeling down with a trusted friend or pastor, and just say, 'These things shouldn't be there. Please help me let God take them away.' Self-examination isn't just about finding things that shouldn't be there. It's also about finding things that are there but have been neglected. That's sometimes where vocation begins. Look inside your heart. Do it. Make a habit of it.

- **Habit number two: pray.**

  Don't get in a pickle about whether to pray with a book or just freestyle: do both. Once a day each. Simple as that. Think about the way you shop. Sometimes I shop with a list; sometimes not. Sometimes it's a pleasure; sometimes it's a necessity; sometimes it's a pain. Sometimes I go with someone else, or even help someone else to go; sometimes I go on my own. Sometimes it's about big things; sometimes it's about little things. Sometimes I really think carefully about it, and check through a kind of recipe list; sometimes I just do it, and realize later what I've forgotten. Prayer's just as varied. Just do it. Make a habit of it.

- **Habit number three: fast.**

  Fasting is about toughening yourself up so you don't go all pathetic at the first smell or sight of something sweet or tasty. It's about making yourself someone to be reckoned with and not a pushover. Make a pattern of life so you don't just drift to the mobile phone or email or internet as a transitional object. Stand in solidarity with those who don't get to choose. If you can't give up a single meal, do you really care about global hunger? And learn how to be really hungry. Hungry for righteousness. Hungry for justice and peace. Hungry, fundamentally, for Easter – hungry for the resurrection only God can bring in Christ. Do it. Make a habit of it.

- **Habit number four: give money away.**

  'Ah,' you may say, 'I'm in a tight spot right now: I don't have any money.' Let me tell you now: there will never be a time in your life when you think it's a good time for giving money away. Try to tie your money to your prayers. Give money to something you believe in, and pray for the organisation you give money to. Just do it. Make a habit of it.

- **Habit number five: read the Bible.**

  Imagine you were going into a crowded airport to meet someone you were longing to see but weren't sure you'd recognize. And imagine you had a photo album of pictures that showed them in a thousand different activities. Wouldn't you study that photo album so you'd almost committed it to memory? That's what the Bible is – a series of portrayals of God, and we study it to get to know God better so we'll have no recognition problems in a crowd. Genesis has 50 chapters: you can almost do it in Lent. You can get through a couple of Paul's letters a week. There's a dozen minor prophets: read a couple a week. Find a nether region in the Bible, and go digging. Buy an accessible commentary and follow a few verses each day. Just do it. Make a habit of it.

- **Habit number six: repair broken relationships.**

  This is the last one and, for many people, the toughest. We've probably, many of us, got one big relationship that's all wrong – and maybe there's not a whole lot we can do about it. Maybe it's just a matter of keeping out of someone's way, if we've done them wrong, or trying to be civil, if they've hurt us. Now may not be the time to make things better. Now may not yet be God's time. But that doesn't mean we let all our other relationships get to that kind of place. Is there someone out there, a sibling, a rival, a long-time friend, a person who always felt inferior to you? Could you write that person a letter this Lent to say some things you've always appreciated about them but you've never told them? You can make it subtle. You can dress it up as something else. But could you see your way to that? And what about people whose names you don't know, people from whom you're estranged without ever having done the damage yourself? Could you make a new friend this Lent? Do it. Make a habit of it.

May you have a holy Lent, rooted and grounded in love.

Samuel Wells

The importance of daily prayer

Daily prayer is a way of sustaining that most special of all relationships. It helps if we want to pray, but it can be sufficient to want to want to pray, or even to want to want to want to pray! The direction of the heart is what matters, not its achievements. Gradually we are shaped and changed by the practice of daily prayer. Apprentices in prayer never graduate, but we become a little bit more the people God wants us to be.

Prayer isn't a technique; it's a relationship, and it starts in the most ordinary, instinctive reactions to everyday life:

- **Gratitude**: good things are always happening to us, however small.
- **Wonder**: we often see amazing things in nature and in people but pass them by.
- **Need**: we bump into scores of needs every day.
- **Sorrow**: we mess up.

Prayer is taking those instincts and stretching them out before God. The rules then are: start small, stay natural, be honest.

Here are four ways of putting some structure around daily prayer.

1 **The Quiet Time**. This is the classic way of reading a passage of the Bible, using Bible reading reflections like those in this book, and then praying naturally about the way the passage has struck you, taking to God the questions, resolutions, hopes, fears and other responses that have arisen within you.

2 **The Daily Office**. This is a structured way of reading Scripture and psalms, and praying for individuals, the world, the day ahead, etc. It keeps us anchored in the Lectionary, the basic reading of the Church, and so ensures that we engage with the breadth of Scripture, rather than just with our favourite passages. It also puts us in living touch with countless others around the world who are doing something similar. There is a simple form of Morning Prayer on pp. 48–49 of this book and a form of Night Prayer (Compline) on pp. 52–55. Fuller forms can be found in *Common Worship: Daily Prayer*.

3   **Holy Reading**. Also known as *Lectio Divina*, this is a tried and trusted way of feeding and meditating on the Bible, described more fully on pages 6–7 of this book. In essence, here is how it is done:

- *Read:* Read the passage slowly until a phrase catches your attention.
- *Reflect:* Chew the phrase carefully, drawing the goodness out of it.
- *Respond:* Pray about the thoughts and feelings that have surfaced in you.
- *Rest:* You may want to rest in silence for a while.
- *Repeat:* Carry on with the passage …

4   **Silence**. In our distracted culture some people are drawn more to silence than to words. This will involve *centring* (hunkering down), *focusing* on a short biblical phrase (e.g. 'Come, Holy Spirit'), *waiting* (repeating the phrase as necessary), and *ending* (perhaps with the Lord's Prayer). The length of time is irrelevant.

There are, of course, as many ways of praying as there are people to pray. There are no right or wrong ways to pray. 'Pray as you can, not as you can't', is wise advice. The most important thing is to make sure there is sufficient structure to keep prayer going when it's a struggle as well as when it's a joy. Prayer is too important to leave to chance.

+John Pritchard

Lectio Divina – a way of reading the Bible

Lectio Divina is a contemplative way of reading the Bible. It dates back to the early centuries of the Christian Church and was established as a monastic practice by Benedict in the 6th century. It is a way of praying the Scriptures that leads us deeper into God's word. We slow down. We read a short passage more than once. We chew it over slowly and carefully. We savour it. Scripture begins to speak to us in a new way. It speaks to us personally, and aids that union we have with God through Christ who is himself the Living Word.

Make sure you are sitting comfortably. Breathe slowly and deeply. Ask God to speak to you through the passage that you are about to read.

This way of praying starts with our silence. We often make the mistake of thinking prayer is about what we say to God. It is actually the other way round. God wants to speak to us. He will do this through the Scriptures. So don't worry about what to say. Don't worry if nothing jumps out at you at first. God is patient. He will wait for the opportunity to get in. He will give you a word and lead you to understand its meaning for you today.

First reading: Listen

As you read the passage listen for a word or phrase that attracts you. Allow it to arise from the passage as if it is God's word for you today. Sit in silence repeating the word or phrase in your head.

Then say the word or phrase aloud.

Second reading: Ponder

As you read the passage again, ask how this word or phrase speaks to your life and why it has connected with you. Ponder it carefully. Don't worry if you get distracted – it may be part of your response to offer to God. Sit in silence and then frame a single sentence that begins to say aloud what this word or phrase says to you.

Third reading: Pray

As you read the passage for the last time, ask what Christ is calling from you. What is it that you need to do or consider or relinquish or take on as a result of what God is saying to you in this word or phrase? In the silence that follows the reading, pray for the grace of the Spirit to plant this word in your heart.

If you are in a group, talk for a few minutes and pray with each other.

If you are on your own, speak your prayer to God either aloud or in the silence of your heart.

If there is time, you may even want to read the passage a fourth time, and then end with the same silence before God with which you began.

+Stephen Cottrell

Lent

Psalm **38**
Daniel 9.3-6, 17-19
1 Timothy 6.6-19

Daniel 9.3-6, 17-19

'O Lord, hear; O Lord, forgive!' (v.19)

At the beginning of Lent, the Church turns back to its origins. Christian life begins in the baptismal font, when we first renounced evil and turned in faith to the Lord. Daniel, the prophet and visionary, shows us the way in today's reading as he repents on behalf of his people, acknowledging their history of sin and rebellion. Repentance is never the outcome of despair, but rather an act of profound hope. Daniel trusts that Jerusalem will be restored. The Lord will shine upon his people once again.

History vindicates Daniel – the book was almost certainly composed long after the time it reflects, when God had brought his people home. As we make confession of our sins this Lent, we do so not as a grovelling act of self-hatred, but as a response to God's mercy. Confession is grounded in clarity about ourselves, a recognition that sin is a consequences of our choices, and that our choices are determined by our desires. So we come home to reality, to the God 'to whom all hearts are open, all desires known, and from whom no secrets are hidden'. God does not lead us to repentance to condemn us but to set us free from all the destructive and acquisitive instincts that crowd in on our lives and erode our faith and humanity. It is an act of trust – our part in the renewal of all creation.

COLLECT

Almighty and everlasting God,
you hate nothing that you have made
and forgive the sins of all those who are penitent:
create and make in us new and contrite hearts
that we, worthily lamenting our sins
and acknowledging our wretchedness,
may receive from you, the God of all mercy,
perfect remission and forgiveness;
through Jesus Christ your Son our Lord,
who is alive and reigns with you,
in the unity of the Holy Spirit,
one God, now and for ever.

Galatians 2.11-end

*'I have been crucified with Christ; and it is no longer I who live,
but it is Christ who lives in me' (vv.19-20)*

We come now to the heart of Paul's despair over his back-sliding converts. He has seen for himself how deep a hold the Jewish law still has on Peter, and how easy it is for gentile converts to be pressured into accepting circumcision and the food laws 'just in case', or to gain approval from others who are doing so.

For Paul, this is a betrayal of the gospel that makes null the saving death of Christ. His language is extreme because something extreme is at stake. Is Christianity another form of Judaism – more open and accessible to gentiles but still requiring the adoption of a distinctly Jewish identity? Or is it something different – a new movement of God to bring the gentiles into the promises God made to the Jews, and yet without requiring conformity to the law? If the second of these is true, then obedience to the law implies radical doubt in the gospel, a sinful abandonment of hope in Christ alone.

In his anguish over the fate of the Galatians, Paul articulates the mystical heart of the gospel. Through his death on the cross, Christ has become the inner life of every believer. Our selfhood is not grounded in our achievements, however worthy, but only in his grace and love.

Holy God,
our lives are laid open before you:
rescue us from the chaos of sin
and through the death of your Son
bring us healing and make us whole
in Jesus Christ our Lord.

COLLECT

Friday 7 March

Psalms **3**, 7 *or* **88** (95)
Genesis 40
Galatians 3.1-14

Galatians 3.1-14

'Did you experience so much for nothing?' (v.4)

Paul is determined to bring the Galatians back to the liberation they initially experienced through his preaching. He now batters them with a series of rhetorical questions. He insists that they review their experience, remembering that it was trust that enabled them to receive the Spirit, and not conformity to the Jewish law. Their former willingness to trust proved that they were genuine children of Abraham, included in the promise God made to him and to all his descendants, even though they were not Jews by birth.

Paul's characteristic theology of grace and faith is drawn out of him by this conflict and crisis; we can see him articulating the principles by which Christians have lived for 2000 years as he struggles to convince his 'foolish' and 'bewitched' converts.

In our time, tolerance is considered a virtue, and Paul's heated argument might be regarded as a form of persuasion close to bullying. Yet there is a challenge for us here. How ready are we to explore our own Christian experience and renew our trust in the fundamentals of our faith? This Lent we have a chance to consider whether the faith we hold is progressively liberating us or imprisoning us. Are we growing in maturity, generosity, charity – or are we becoming embittered, fearful, cynical? Has Christ indeed redeemed us from 'the curse of the law'?

COLLECT

Almighty and everlasting God,
you hate nothing that you have made
and forgive the sins of all those who are penitent:
create and make in us new and contrite hearts
that we, worthily lamenting our sins
and acknowledging our wretchedness,
may receive from you, the God of all mercy,
perfect remission and forgiveness;
through Jesus Christ your Son our Lord,
who is alive and reigns with you,
in the unity of the Holy Spirit,
one God, now and for ever.

Psalms **71** *or* 96, **97**, 100
Genesis 41.1-24
Galatians 3.15-22

Galatians 3.15-22

'Why then the law?' (v.19)

Now comes Paul's most radical theological innovation in this letter. He compares God's promises to Abraham and his offspring to a will that cannot be legally altered. He then suggests, daringly, that God's promise was not directed to the plurality of Abraham's descendants, but rather to the one descendant who sums up in his person the whole of Israel's faith, Jesus Christ. This is startling enough, but the concept of God's promise as a 'will' enables Paul to put the law in a secondary place. The promise came first. The law was added centuries later in the time of Moses as a restraining force, to keep lawlessness under control, until the 'offspring' to whom the promise was made was born.

This argument is more fully stated in the letter to the Romans, but here it enables Paul to reassert the primacy of the gospel over the law without denying that the law was given by God. How are we to understand this? Law is a social good and gives us a moral code. We need constraint and convention. But these have their limits. Even the best laws cannot of themselves set us free from the attitudes and habits that lead to sin. Law cannot save us from death or give us hope in life eternal. But the promise, given originally to Abraham, and vindicated in Christ's death and resurrection, is there for us today and always.

Holy God,
our lives are laid open before you:
rescue us from the chaos of sin
and through the death of your Son
bring us healing and make us whole
in Jesus Christ our Lord.

COLLECT

Monday 10 March

Galatians 3.23 – 4.7

'So you are no longer a slave but ... an heir' (4.7)

Paul wants his listeners to have a grown-up faith. He wants them to move on from being a slave to being an heir, from minor to major, and he uses all sorts of images and arguments in these chapters to make the point. Paul did his theology on the run, but what rings through his writing all the time is the theme of freedom. He has experienced the power of religion to imprison us in small spaces under the control of rulebooks, and he aches for his converts to know the liberation of a Christ-centred life.

Distorted religion can still clip our wings. The big move forward for me was the realization that faith was not about regulating my life but about relishing a relationship. I had many of the pieces of the Christian jigsaw lying around but they had seemed obscure and opaque. What was this piece for, and that one? (I thought the same about maths). When I found the liberating piece of the jigsaw that described a relationship with Christ, everything began to make sense – and what's more, every other relationship was transformed as well. 'There is no longer Jew or Greek ... slave or free ... male and female ...' (3.28). We've been working on that ever since.

How, I wonder, will we claim and live that freedom today?

COLLECT

Almighty God,
whose Son Jesus Christ fasted forty days in the wilderness,
and was tempted as we are, yet without sin:
give us grace to discipline ourselves in obedience to your Spirit;
and, as you know our weakness,
so may we know your power to save;
through Jesus Christ your Son our Lord,
who is alive and reigns with you,
in the unity of the Holy Spirit,
one God, now and for ever.

Psalms **44** *or* **106*** (or 103)
Genesis 41.46 – 42.5
Galatians 4.8-20

Galatians 4.8-20

'... until Christ is formed in you' (v.19)

The strain on Paul is beginning to show. The believers in Galatia were being disturbed by Jewish Christians who wanted to turn the clock back and put the gentile converts back into a cage of rules and regulations 'observing special days, and months, and seasons' (v.10). 'How can you want to be enslaved again?' (v.9) is his anguished retort – 'I am afraid that my work for you may have been wasted' (v.11).

God always has a bigger vision for us to pursue. We always try to limit the gospel, to tame the tiger into a domestic pet. But (to change the image) God constantly gives us clothes that are two sizes too big for us, inviting us to grow into them and to experience the beauty and risk of a world infused with God's life and love. With God there is always more – more hope, more opportunity, more justice, more joy. Always a bigger vision. It's summed up in an extraordinary group of words: the vision is that 'Christ is formed in you' (v.19). That's a staggering image if you think about it: that the character of Christ himself should become a reality in our own confused and divided lives.

And the point Paul wants to make is as important now as it was then: if that's what God wants for us, how can we settle for anything less?

Heavenly Father,
your Son battled with the powers of darkness,
and grew closer to you in the desert:
help us to use these days to grow in wisdom and prayer
that we may witness to your saving love
in Jesus Christ our Lord.

COLLECT

Wednesday 12 March

Galatians 4.21 – 5.1

'For freedom Christ has set us free' (5.1)

Paul relentlessly pursues his theme. Nothing will stop his determination to cry freedom. Now he draws in the two mothers of Abraham's sons, Hagar and Sarah, and uses them as an allegory of two covenants, one leading to slavery and the other to freedom. Everything is fair game as Paul uses argument after argument to beseech the Galatians not to give up the freedom they have in Christ.

A member of my family was once told she couldn't have a position of responsibility in a church because of an improbable reading of something Paul had written in a very specific context. The church leader seemed to be suggesting that Paul was establishing another set of rules, having just released the gentiles from the previous set. As if! Paul specifically says: 'For freedom Christ has set us free' (5.1). The freedom of Christ and the new creation is one of the most important interpretative principles to employ when we're trying to understand and work with difficult biblical material.

The gospel continues to be too good to be true for many (perhaps all) of us. We think we really must put in a few health and safety measures to make the teaching of Jesus manageable. The radical nature of the freedom of Christ is a constant challenge, both a golden promise and an alarming threat.

What will this freedom look like for each of us today? Even better, what will it feel like?

COLLECT

Almighty God,
whose Son Jesus Christ fasted forty days in the wilderness,
and was tempted as we are, yet without sin:
give us grace to discipline ourselves in obedience to your Spirit;
and, as you know our weakness,
so may we know your power to save;
through Jesus Christ your Son our Lord,
who is alive and reigns with you,
in the unity of the Holy Spirit,
one God, now and for ever.

Psalms **42**, 43 *or* 113, **115**
Genesis 42.18-28
Galatians 5.2-15

Galatians 5.2-15

'Christ will be of no benefit to you' (v.2)

This is where we reach the high (or low) point of Paul's irritation. He's tried every argument and now decides to throw in a few threats. 'If you let yourselves be circumcised, Christ will be of no benefit to you … [you] have cut yourselves off from Christ' (vv.2,4). He even gets to the point of wishing his opponents would castrate themselves – not a conventional strategy in pastoral care. All of this shows just how important it is that the Galatian believers don't fall back into a legalistic understanding of faith.

We've travelled so far beyond this particular battle over circumcision that the argument seems almost amusingly arcane to us, but to Paul it was deadly serious. The whole integrity of a faith based on grace was at stake. Truth mattered. The ferocity of Paul's concern ought to give us pause and make us ask how much truth matters to us. There is an urgent explanatory task in our culture, and it often seems that as a Church we're not well equipped for it. Questions about belief in God, the nature of reality, science and faith, suffering, other faiths, etc., are all around us, yet often we duck the conversation, fearing our inadequacy.

If the truth isn't something both to defend and to commend, then we slide into a situation where nothing really matters very much – and nothing is worth either living for or dying for. That way lies tyranny and catastrophe. Paul recognized the danger. Do we?

Heavenly Father,
your Son battled with the powers of darkness,
and grew closer to you in the desert:
help us to use these days to grow in wisdom and prayer
that we may witness to your saving love
in Jesus Christ our Lord.

COLLECT

Friday 14 March

Galatians 5.16-end

'If we live by the Spirit, let us also be guided by the Spirit' (v.25)

In trying to demonstrate what's distinctive about the way Christians should live, Paul sets two approaches in clear opposition: the way of the flesh and the way of the Spirit. By 'flesh', Paul doesn't quite mean what we might think; he means more like 'the way of the world', a world without Christ as the touchstone. As ever, Paul pulls no punches: those who live in a worldly way will not inherit the kingdom of God. Your choice, he says.

It's well on occasions to see the contrast laid out starkly, but the practice of 'splitting', if it becomes a habit, can lead to some pretty unpleasant behaviour – condemnation, judgementalism, etc. But Paul shows us the better way – live by the Spirit and be guided by the Spirit. If you're lost in a car in a strange town, what you need isn't a list of complicated instructions but someone who knows the place well and who'll get in the front seat beside you and talk you through the road system. We have such a guide, says Paul, the Spirit of Jesus Christ, who will ensure that we choose the streets that are marked by love, joy, peace, patience, kindness, generosity and so on. So the question is: which navigation system do we use? Are we nudged and guided by the Spirit, or by the compulsions and obsessions of the world?

Will we start each day by inviting the divine Guide to show us the way?

COLLECT

Almighty God,
whose Son Jesus Christ fasted forty days in the wilderness,
and was tempted as we are, yet without sin:
give us grace to discipline ourselves in obedience to your Spirit;
and, as you know our weakness,
so may we know your power to save;
through Jesus Christ your Son our Lord,
who is alive and reigns with you,
in the unity of the Holy Spirit,
one God, now and for ever.

Psalms 59, **63** *or* 120, **121**, 122
Genesis 43.1-15
Galatians 6

Galatians 6

*'May I never boast of anything except the cross of our Lord
Jesus Christ' (v.14)*

The final chapter of this anguished letter feels like the final rumblings
of a volcano that's now dying down. Paul's impassioned warnings still
appear every so often – 'Do not be deceived; God is not mocked …'
(v.7), 'they want you to be circumcised so that they may boast …'
(v.13) – but he's beginning to relax and to return to his most
compelling themes of the power of the cross and the reality of the
new creation (vv.14,15).

And he alludes to the most mysterious sign of his identification with
Jesus Christ – the stigmata, for 'I carry the marks of Jesus branded on
my body' (v.17). A few saints through history seem to have been
marked in this way, Francis of Assisi and Padre Pio among them. If
someone dwells on the cross and lives in its shadow for long enough,
perhaps they begin to replicate some of its features. It won't be the
case for most of us, but when we read this tiny clue at the end of
Paul's letter we might begin to understand why he was so passionate
about maintaining the distinctiveness and truth of the gospel.

At one time I thought the Christian faith was a 'take it or leave it'
option, mainly for the seriously religious. Now I believe it to be the
pearl of great price, the most valuable thing that this world affords.
But, as Lent gets under way, how close to the cross do I dare get?

Heavenly Father,
your Son battled with the powers of darkness,
and grew closer to you in the desert:
help us to use these days to grow in wisdom and prayer
that we may witness to your saving love
in Jesus Christ our Lord.

COLLECT

Hebrews 1

'... in these last days he has spoken to us by a Son' (v.2)

If you've got a main point to make, you might as well make it early. That's what the writer to the Hebrews does. He wants to make it clear that whatever other means God has used to reconcile heaven and earth in the past (angels, the sacrificial system, etc.) the full and final word has been spoken through a Son who is 'the exact imprint of God's very being' (v.3). The writer heaps on the superlatives, tossing in as an aside that it was through the Son that God also created the universe.

The main comparison that he makes in the early chapters is between what the angels do and what the Son does. This may not be something that keeps many of us awake at night now, but in the Jewish culture for which Hebrews is written, this was an important comparison. And it asks us how adequate our own understanding of Jesus Christ actually is. Is there a danger that we reduce him to a strolling minstrel, spinning tales of peace and love in the Galilean hills? Do we play down the divinity in order to make him manageable for a sceptical age? If so, reading the letter to the Hebrews is like a face-full of cold water. Prepare to meet an exalted Christ. Prepare to encounter a divine Son worthy of our wonder and allegiance.

And yet he goes with us this very day. Trust him.

COLLECT

Almighty God,
you show to those who are in error the light of your truth,
that they may return to the way of righteousness:
grant to all those who are admitted
    into the fellowship of Christ's religion,
that they may reject those things
    that are contrary to their profession,
and follow all such things as are agreeable to the same;
through our Lord Jesus Christ,
who is alive and reigns with you,
in the unity of the Holy Spirit,
one God, now and for ever.

Hebrews 2.1-9

*'... we must pay greater attention
... so that we do not drift away' (v.1)*

The writer introduces us to another great theme of his letter – that his Jewish Christian readers must be careful not to drift back into Jewish practice. The message received through angels was important enough; how much more the message received through Jesus, 'who for a little while was made lower than the angels' but is now 'crowned with glory and honour because of the suffering of death' (v.9). Christ is the final word; you'd better believe it, says the writer. Don't drift.

It's very easy for our faith to drift. I was on holiday recently and realized at the end that I hadn't said my daily prayers all week. Not that I felt out of touch with God as I celebrated family, rest, playfulness, nature and more. But I realized that the discipline of prayer by which I put such store had fallen apart almost without my noticing. A professional musician may neglect practice for a day or two but after a week audiences would begin to notice.

'Therefore we must pay greater attention' says the writer (v.1), not because of some blind requirement but because of the damage that neglect of our core relationship with God may cause. As a Christian I'm only as effective as I allow God's Spirit to make me. On my own I'm like a fish left high and dry on the beach, out of my normal habitat and running out of breath.

So beware – problems often start small but grow big.

Almighty God,
by the prayer and discipline of Lent
may we enter into the mystery of Christ's sufferings,
and by following in his Way
come to share in his glory;
through Jesus Christ our Lord.

COLLECT

Wednesday 19 March

Joseph of Nazareth

Psalms 25, 147.1-12
Isaiah 11.1-10
Matthew 13.54-end

Isaiah 11.1-10

'They will not hurt or destroy on all my holy mountain' (v.9)

'The wolf shall live with the lamb,' says Isaiah (v.6), but you can guarantee the lamb won't get much sleep. Or not in the world as it is. But Isaiah is looking beyond the violence and dysfunctionality of our present world order to the peaceable kingdom where God's just and gentle rule holds all things in harmony. Isaiah has just been telling Judah and Assyria that their number is up, but he can see through the veil to another order where the world will be full of the knowledge of the Lord, and God's peace will at last soak into everything.

There's a long tradition of secular kingdom-building and an equally long history of utopian dreams that come down in flames. But the Judaeo/Christian tradition is shaped not around flawed humanity but around the perfect character of God. I'm a willing worker for the kingdom, but I'm not trusting my plans to be more than scratches made on the back of an envelope with a blunt stick. God's purpose is beyond anything that the biblical writers, or Bunyan, or Lewis, or Tolkien could have imagined, even with the help of angels. Just occasionally we glimpse what Joseph must have glimpsed as he worked alongside his Son. That young man might have been making furniture, but he was preparing to design heaven.

I want to be in his team.

COLLECT

God our Father,
who from the family of your servant David
raised up Joseph the carpenter
to be the guardian of your incarnate Son
and husband of the Blessed Virgin Mary:
give us grace to follow him
in faithful obedience to your commands;
through Jesus Christ your Son our Lord,
who is alive and reigns with you,
in the unity of the Holy Spirit,
one God, now and for ever.

Psalms **34** *or* **143**, 146
Genesis 45.1-15
Hebrews 3.1-6

Hebrews 3.1-6

'Christ ... was faithful over God's house as a Son' (v.6)

You don't have to remember the epic film *The Ten Commandments* to know that Moses was a colossal figure in Jewish history. He faced up to Pharaoh and led the Israelite charge out of captivity in Egypt, and then he guided his awkward people through years of painful learning in the desert. In the meantime he enjoyed the most extraordinary intimacy with God.

But Moses, for all his distinction, was as nothing compared to the Son, the young man from Galilee. Like Moses in the desert, Jesus was 'faithful over God's house', the little band of loyal disciples who were to be the new Israel, the Church. So now we are God's house, the royal household who have the privilege of belonging to the Son. I wonder if we grasp the dimensions of this privilege? Even coming to church on a Sunday is an amazing honour – to be invited to soak in the Spirit of Jesus, to feed at his table, to spend time with friends of the Friend. Sadly, too often we just roll up by habit and expect some passable Christian event called a service.

Moses came out of God's presence with his face glowing. Might not we open ourselves to the same glory?

Almighty God,
you show to those who are in error the light of your truth,
that they may return to the way of righteousness:
grant to all those who are admitted
into the fellowship of Christ's religion,
that they may reject those things
that are contrary to their profession,
and follow all such things as are agreeable to the same;
through our Lord Jesus Christ,
who is alive and reigns with you,
in the unity of the Holy Spirit,
one God, now and for ever.

COLLECT

Friday 21 March

Psalms 40, **41** *or* 142, **144**
Genesis 45.16-end
Hebrews 3.7-end

Hebrews 3.7-end

'Today, if you hear his voice, do not harden your hearts' (vv.7-8)

The image of a hard heart is a vivid one. We've probably all seen a heart on TV, fleshy, beating, and very much alive. A 'hard heart' or a 'heart of stone' is the complete antithesis of such a picture. The writer to the Hebrews is concerned that his readers don't suffer spiritual arteriosclerosis, as did the Israelites following God through the desert and wondering if this was all folly.

We too can suffer from heart disease if we allow the gospel's supple grace to slide into the law's hardened requirements. When that happens, people lose faith in religion – they see faith getting trapped in restrictive practices and our small minds fearing the rampant freedom of God. A religion of rules and regulations is hardly going to get people leaping out of bed on a Sunday morning. The answer lies in that evocative phrase: 'Today, if you hear his voice …' The voice of God is rarely loud but it's quietly persistent, and it always invites us to a faith that's deeper, richer, more liquid and more adventurous than our human religious constructs.

Behind and within every event of today will be that deep voice which we might hear with the warm pleasure of recognition, 'if we do not harden our hearts'.

COLLECT

Almighty God,
you show to those who are in error the light of your truth,
that they may return to the way of righteousness:
grant to all those who are admitted
    into the fellowship of Christ's religion,
that they may reject those things
    that are contrary to their profession,
and follow all such things as are agreeable to the same;
through our Lord Jesus Christ,
who is alive and reigns with you,
in the unity of the Holy Spirit,
one God, now and for ever.

Psalms 3, **25** *or* **147**
Genesis 46.1-7, 28-end
Hebrews 4.1-13

Hebrews 4.1-13

'... the promise of entering his rest is still open' (v.1)

When you're writing Bible reflections late at night – again – you find yourself much attracted to the promise that God's rest is still open. But that rest is much deeper than merely a better organized life. It's the rest of God after the massive work of creation. It's the rest sought by the wandering people of Israel in a land of promise. It's the rest summed up in that beautiful word *shalom*, meaning harmony, peace, fulfilment, wholeness. It's the eternal rest we have in God.

But 'today' that rest is available again. Why? Because of Jesus. There's both tenderness and warning in this passage. The writer is desperate that his readers don't harden their hearts and disobey the heavenly vision, because the opportunity to enter their inheritance, their rest, is right there before them.

We might not live in such fear and trepidation in our day, but this promised rest in God can still be missed if we're not careful. We can be so Christian we fail to follow Christ. We can be so familiar with the good news that we fail to live it. We can be so confident of our faith that we forget to use it. When a small child from our church school saw me in a cassock, she said: 'Mr Pritchard, are you pretending to be a vicar?' The question has gone deep.

God's glorious rest is available today, but will we enter it?

> Almighty God,
> by the prayer and discipline of Lent
> may we enter into the mystery of Christ's sufferings,
> and by following in his Way
> come to share in his glory;
> through Jesus Christ our Lord.

COLLECT

23

Monday 24 March

Hebrews 4.14 – 5.10

'... so that we may receive mercy and find grace' (4.16)

From cool to warm, today's passage acts like a pivot point for the whole of the letter to the Hebrews, an early (possibly 60s AD) community of Jewish followers of the Messiah Jesus, probably somewhere in the eastern part of the Roman Empire. The writer has been advocating the uniqueness of Jesus with particular reference to the temple system of priesthood and sacrifice – and will develop that argument later in the letter. At times, to our hearing at least, the argument can seem technical, rational and even cool. But here the rational argument gives way to warmth and tenderness.

The humanity of those receiving the letter is recognized. And the high priest Jesus is not just being acclaimed for his sufficiency in the great act of salvation. He is, through it all, revealed to be compassionate and good. He is the One to whom we can come 'with boldness' to receive all the mercy and find all the grace we need. And so today, wherever we are, the gospel – the good news – of Jesus the Christ needs to be experienced exactly as that, as good news, as mercy and grace. However 'correct' or brilliant our understanding of theology, the Jesus path must above all be lived and shared as a life of tenderness and compassion. So may you receive from him all the mercy and grace you need for this day!

COLLECT

Almighty God,
whose most dear Son went not up to joy but first he suffered pain,
and entered not into glory before he was crucified:
mercifully grant that we, walking in the way of the cross,
may find it none other than the way of life and peace;
through Jesus Christ your Son our Lord,
who is alive and reigns with you,
in the unity of the Holy Spirit,
one God, now and for ever.

Psalms 111, 113
1 Samuel 2.1-10
Romans 5.12-end

Annunciation of Our Lord
to the Blessed Virgin Mary

Romans 5.12-end

'... by the one man's obedience the many will be made righteous'
(v.19)

You can help to change the world for good today. In this part of his inspiring letter to the first Church in Rome, Paul is highlighting how the actions of one person can change everything. Specifically, he is contrasting the actions of Adam, the archetypal human from the great Jewish story of beginnings – and, says Paul, the one through whom sin, judgement and death came into the world – with the actions of Jesus the Christ, the One through whom has come grace, justification and life 'abounding for the many' (v.15).

On this Day of the Annunciation, we celebrate the actions of another *one person changing everything*. Mary's brilliant and beautiful 'let it be' to the angel Gabriel's astonishing message both anticipates and makes possible the coming into the world of the One who will bring grace and life. Mary's grace opens up the way for the grace-filled Christ to become one of us, one with us, and so to change everything. This pattern and possibility continues for us now. The decisions we are called to make today, while probably being far more 'ordinary' than that which was asked of Mary, may also change the world! May we have the courage to say with Mary, 'let it be with me according to your word' (Luke 1.38)!

We beseech you, O Lord,
pour your grace into our hearts,
that as we have known the incarnation of your Son Jesus Christ
by the message of an angel,
so by his cross and passion
we may be brought to the glory of his resurrection;
through Jesus Christ your Son our Lord,
who is alive and reigns with you,
in the unity of the Holy Spirit,
one God, now and for ever.

COLLECT

Wednesday 26 March

Psalm **38** *or* **119.1-32**
Genesis 49.1-32
Hebrews 6.13-end

Hebrews 6.13-end

'We have this hope ...' (v.19)

Where we do go when the pressure is on and everything threatens to overwhelm us? The letter to the Hebrews, like most of the letters in our New Testament, is written to a community of Christ-followers who are under some kind of pressure. It's not clear what form the particular pressure was taking in the case of this small church community, but it is clear that those pressures had led some to 'fall away' from the faith. For a movement constantly under suspicion and threat, this was a particularly serious matter.

This is the backdrop to the writer's great declaration of hope in Jesus, who has gone this way before us, undergoing similar trials and emerging faithful to his calling. This hope is, the writer says, 'a sure and steadfast anchor of the soul' (v.19). Anchors may be some way from most of our daily experience, but the picture is clear. Our hope in Jesus will be enough, should we entrust ourselves to it, to hold us when everything gets rough and threatens to overwhelm us, even (and particularly) in the toughness of Lent. Vitally, this is not hope in a concept, a creed or even the Church. It is hope rooted in a person, in the One who promises: 'I am with you always, to the end of the age' (Matthew 28.20). We have this hope!

COLLECT

Almighty God,
whose most dear Son went not up to joy but first he suffered pain,
and entered not into glory before he was crucified:
mercifully grant that we, walking in the way of the cross,
may find it none other than the way of life and peace;
through Jesus Christ your Son our Lord,
who is alive and reigns with you,
in the unity of the Holy Spirit,
one God, now and for ever.

Psalms **56**, 57 *or* 14, **15**, 16*
Genesis 49.33 – end of 50
Hebrews 7.1-10

Hebrews 7.1-10

'... but resembling the Son of God' (v.3)

What words might people choose to describe you in this season of your life? And whom do you resemble? In this passage in the Letter to the Hebrews, the writer is working with connections between Jesus and a famous figure from the beginning of the story of the Hebrew people, the fabled King Melchizedek of Salem, who blessed Abraham when the latter was returning from a victorious battle. There's a technical aspect to the argument that is developed, around greatness, order and rank. But perhaps more interesting from our perspective is the idea that emerges of likeness to another. Melchizedek, says the writer, resembles the Son of God (who we may take to represent the God-man Jesus).

What does this likeness look like? Two words are used to describe the character of the likeness shared between Melchizedek and Jesus the Christ. They are 'righteousness' and 'peace' (v.2) – two words that appear in close proximity in the Jewish Scriptures (Isaiah 60.17). If we are to resemble Jesus at all, perhaps these two words – and the ideas that have emerged around them from our living with the Jesus story – might be very good places to begin. To bring righteousness and peace to others in the name of Jesus, we need first to become people of righteousness and peace ourselves. So what might it look like for us to be people of righteousness and peace today?

Eternal God,
give us insight
to discern your will for us,
to give up what harms us,
and to seek the perfection we are promised
in Jesus Christ our Lord.

COLLECT

Friday 28 March

Hebrews 7.11-end

'Now if perfection had been attainable ...' (v.11)

Could anything be better than perfect? In this part of the letter to the Hebrews, the writer suggests that the sacrificial system of the levitical priesthood can only go so far in its making right of what is wrong. Something else is needed. And only the coming of the One who 'through the power of an indestructible life' (v.16) and 'who has been made perfect forever' (v.28) can truly bring salvation (v.25). Perfection clearly means a lot in the context of this letter, its author and the community to whom it was written; in our own context, the idea of perfection may need careful handling.

One of the wonderful characteristics of the Jesus path is the sense that it is not a ladder of achievement. It's not just for the most brilliant and the most committed, nor the most perfect of disciples. Rather, it's a new call each day to every one of us, in all our mess and wonder, to step into the way of Jesus, and to adopt a continual life of orientation towards him, and to move in his direction. Of course we should aim to be as righteous and as peaceful as we possibly can be! And we are made perfect – in the perfection of Christ. In the light of that beautiful gift, our call is to live each day with grace and mercy, peace and righteousness. May that re-orientation resume today!

Almighty God,
whose most dear Son went not up to joy but first he suffered pain,
and entered not into glory before he was crucified:
mercifully grant that we, walking in the way of the cross,
may find it none other than the way of life and peace;
through Jesus Christ your Son our Lord,
who is alive and reigns with you,
in the unity of the Holy Spirit,
one God, now and for ever.

Psalms **31** *or* 20, 21, **23**
Exodus 1.22 – 2.10
Hebrews 8

Hebrews 8

'for they shall all know me' (v.11)

Rules or relationship? In today's passage, the writer acclaims the better nature of the new covenant that the coming of Jesus the Christ has brought to the world. This covenant will transcend the keeping of rules and the making of sacrifices. Keeping the laws of the new covenant will become our instinct, not our duty, and the writer portrays God as saying of his people, 'I will put my laws in their minds, and write them on their hearts' (v.10). We'll do the right thing not because we are being forced to, but because it is our deepest, and God-given, intuition.

This picture that the writer gives us of the relationship between God and God's people is one of intimacy. We will be moving away from a behaviour- and rules-based relationship towards a relationship characterized by love. 'I will be their God, and they shall be my people' (v.10) says God and, coming to the intimate core of this new relationship 'they shall all know me' (v.11). This is an encouragement to us to open ourselves up to the possibility of a more intimate and personal relationship with God. So may our prayer and action today be permeated with a sense of the loving presence of the Holy Trinity, as close as breathing. May we come to 'know the Lord' – and to be known ...

Eternal God,
give us insight
to discern your will for us,
to give up what harms us,
and to seek the perfection we are promised
in Jesus Christ our Lord.

COLLECT

Monday 31 March

Psalms 70, **77** or 27, **30**
Exodus 2.11-22
Hebrews 9.1-14

Hebrews 9.1-14

'... this is called the Holy Place' (v.2)

Are there still holy places? In this section of the letter to the Hebrews, the writer is contrasting the elaborate arrangements made for creating a holy place in which sacrifices for sin could be made under the old covenant – with 'cherubim of glory overshadowing the mercy-seat' (v.5) – with the new covenant under which Jesus 'entered once for all into the Holy Place' (v.12) to make the sacrifice that can never be repeated. It's as if Christ himself has become the Holy Place. And he is with us, and he is everywhere.

So are there still holy places? Many of us have an instinct that some places have a tangible feeling of holiness. A medieval church building can feel prayed in. The open moor can seem full of the Creator's presence. And on the holy islands around our shores (including, of course, the Holy Island of Lindisfarne), we can sense the 'thin' quality of the setting and the presence of the saints. So can these places be holy? I think they can – but perhaps what's going on is that their particular holiness is a gift to show us that all places are holy, and that the Christ can be found in every place. So wherever you are today, may you sense the holiness of each place you are in, and the presence of Jesus the Christ, *the Holy Place*.

COLLECT

Merciful Lord,
absolve your people from their offences,
that through your bountiful goodness
we may all be delivered from the chains of those sins
which by our frailty we have committed;
grant this, heavenly Father,
for Jesus Christ's sake, our blessed Lord and Saviour,
who is alive and reigns with you,
in the unity of the Holy Spirit,
one God, now and for ever.

Psalms 54, **79** *or* 32, **36**
Exodus 2.23 – 3.20
Hebrews 9.15-end

Hebrews 9.15-end

'... sketches of the heavenly things' (v.23)

It's understandable to become frustrated and even angry with the way that we behave as a Church. Our mixed motives, worrying hypocrisies and lack of holiness (and our own individual part in all this!) can cause us to lose faith in the community that we call home and which the Christ loves. Our failure so often to be a true sign of the kingdom of God breaking in and breaking out is a thing of deep regret. So what are we to do about the Church (and about us!)? It may be that we can learn from a line in today's passage in the letter to the Hebrews: 'It was necessary' the writer says, 'for the sketches of the heavenly things to be purified with these rites' (v.23).

The initial workings for an artwork are often rough. We and the Church are just 'sketches of the heavenly things'. In the light of this we need to be serious about our discipleship, and to work hard in whichever ways we can to help shape the Church to become more pure in its life, starting of course with ourselves. But perhaps also it's time to give the Church (and ourselves) some breathing space. We are just the first lines of a sketch being drawn for a picture. In the care of the great artist that picture will, in time, become the wonderful artwork it is destined to be.

Merciful Lord,
you know our struggle to serve you:
when sin spoils our lives
and overshadows our hearts,
come to our aid
and turn us back to you again;
through Jesus Christ our Lord.

COLLECT

Wednesday 2 April

Psalms 63, **90** or **34**
Exodus 4.1-23
Hebrews 10.1-18

Hebrews 10.1-18

'I will remember their sins and their lawless deeds no more' (v.17)

Sin is so boring. In this passage from the letter to the Hebrews, the writer pictures God as saying that the time of sin and sacrifice is over. Actually the writer comes close to indicating that God seems to be tired of the whole business of sin and sacrifice repeating itself *ad infinitum*. The law and its consequences are, says the writer, just a shadow of the good things to come. In the meantime, we seem to be stuck with an endless round of shame and blame. I remember hearing a priest in the tradition of hearing confession once saying that there's nothing quite as boring as people's sins.

Bored with sin and its consequences? Or full of compassion and hope? Either way – or both – God finally says 'I will remember their sins and their lawless deeds no more' (v.17). So how might this shape us today? It may be a reminder to us of the boring nature of our sin. If so, let's become a whole lot more imaginative and start to seek out very good things to do! And if someone has sinned against us (again), perhaps the time has come to enjoy the freedom of remembering their lawless deeds no more.

Sin is so boring. Let's become imaginative – let's start doing good!

COLLECT

Merciful Lord,
absolve your people from their offences,
that through your bountiful goodness
we may all be delivered from the chains of those sins
which by our frailty we have committed;
grant this, heavenly Father,
for Jesus Christ's sake, our blessed Lord and Saviour,
who is alive and reigns with you,
in the unity of the Holy Spirit,
one God, now and for ever.

Psalms 53, **86** *or* **37***
Exodus 4.27 – 6.1
Hebrews 10.19-25

Hebrews 10.19-25

*'... let us consider how to provoke one another to love
and good deeds' (v.24)*

Time to get provocative? At this point in the letter to the Hebrews,
the writer goes up a gear, urging the readers to redouble their
efforts to be Christ's people, seeking God with boldness – 'let us
approach with a true heart in full assurance of faith' (v.22) – and
making a difference in the world. The writer's suggestion is that we
should 'provoke one another to love and good deeds' (v.24). In the
context of the particular first-century Christian community receiving
this letter, those acts of love and good deeds might have been both
effective and dangerous.

There has perhaps never been a better time to provoke one another,
in Christ's name, to love and good deeds. Our world is as needy as
ever for goodness and love, and the means to do this are at our
fingertips. The presence of social media and the accessibility of the
internet mean that we can very easily play our part in the ushering
in of the peaceful kingdom of Jesus. One challenge may be around
deciding where exactly we get involved. Another might be in
learning to be generous to others who don't share our particular
passion. The vital thing is to be open to the acts of love and
goodness to which we are being called – and in our provocation
itself, to be full of love and goodness.

Merciful Lord,
you know our struggle to serve you:
when sin spoils our lives
and overshadows our hearts,
come to our aid
and turn us back to you again;
through Jesus Christ our Lord.

COLLECT

Friday 4 April

Psalms **102** *or* **31**
Exodus 6.2-13
Hebrews 10.26-end

Hebrews 10.26-end

'Do not, therefore, abandon that confidence of yours...' (v.35)

We are going to focus on the positive ending to this passage from the letter to the Hebrews. But first a thought on the opening part of today's passage, which threatens terrible judgement on anyone who 'willfully persists in sin' (v.26). Context is always important, and in the early Church any abandonment of the faith had implications not just for the individual but potentially for the whole community. This may account for the severity of the warning to the persistent sinner. Of course, the Church of this time had probably yet to hear the long-pondered conclusions of the likes of Jesus' young disciple John, who came to believe that *God is love*. Even so, we need to hear uncomfortable texts like this and let them question us. Lent is a powerful time in which to let these Scriptures do their work.

If the first part of the passage is a (very big) stick, the ending is more encouraging. 'Do not,' says the writer 'therefore, abandon that confidence of yours; it brings a great reward' (v.35). Sometimes we just need to go back to whatever drew us first to the compassionate Christ and his path – and give ourselves to him again. He is the source of our hope and endurance, and he is our reward. The One who says 'follow me' also says 'I am with you always' (Matthew 28.20).

COLLECT

Merciful Lord,
absolve your people from their offences,
that through your bountiful goodness
we may all be delivered from the chains of those sins
which by our frailty we have committed;
grant this, heavenly Father,
for Jesus Christ's sake, our blessed Lord and Saviour,
who is alive and reigns with you,
in the unity of the Holy Spirit,
one God, now and for ever.

Hebrews 11.1-16

'... and he set out, not knowing where he was going' (v.8)

Joy and fear perhaps, in equal measure. We do not know, of course, what it must have been like to have been part of a Jesus-following community in the 40 years after ascension. We don't know the joy of meeting people who may have known Jesus or his disciples face to face. Nor do most of us experience the kind of fear that went with being part of a persecuted religious sect in the Roman Empire. But the journey through Lent is always a reminder that, like Abraham and the other great figures of faith recorded in this passage from Hebrews, we travel 'not knowing where we are going' (v.8).

The basis for this astonishing faith, as described in the letter, is revealing. The letter-writer meditates on the creation story and sees 'that what is seen was made from things that are not visible' (v.3). So our lives take physical shape as we trust ourselves to the unseen processes of God's creating and sustaining. Whatever you face at this time, may this be an encouragement to you to set out (or to keep on) the path that you sense is your calling from God, especially if the destination seems unclear. It may turn out that the journey will be in itself a gift, producing in you a mature life of faith oriented towards Jesus, who is with you all the way.

Merciful Lord,
you know our struggle to serve you:
when sin spoils our lives
and overshadows our hearts,
come to our aid
and turn us back to you again;
through Jesus Christ our Lord.

COLLECT

Hebrews 11.17-31

'By faith the people passed through the Red sea as if…' (v.29)

Two small words – 'as if' – that are used in common parlance to mock what sounds an unlikely idea ('*as if* there could ever be peace in the world') but in the gospel show the attitude of mind that marks the people who follow the God of the promise. Abraham, Isaac, Jacob, Joseph, Moses and Rahab all faced situations where the promise seemed hopelessly unlikely of fulfilment.

How could Abraham's descendants fill the earth without his only son, Isaac? How could Joseph's people inhabit the land that God had promised them when they had made their home in Egypt? How would Rahab escape the sword of the invading army while her city was being destroyed? How do we maintain our faith in God and God's great purposes of love for us when so much around us seems to deny the reliability of the promise and the possibility of its fulfilment?

The people of Israel making their way to the Promised Land show us how to live and act by faith. They passed through the Red Sea 'as if it were dry land' (v.29). When faced with seemingly insuperable obstacles to the fulfilment of God's purposes, we are called to trust that, from the perspective of divine providence, they are not the end of the road to God's kingdom but the route to it.

COLLECT

Most merciful God,
who by the death and resurrection of your Son Jesus Christ
delivered and saved the world:
grant that by faith in him who suffered on the cross
we may triumph in the power of his victory;
through Jesus Christ your Son our Lord,
who is alive and reigns with you,
in the unity of the Holy Spirit,
one God, now and for ever.

Psalms **35**, 123 *or* **48**, 52
Exodus 8.20-end
Hebrews 11.32 – 12.2

Hebrews 11.32 – 12.2

'... looking to Jesus the pioneer and perfecter of our faith' (12.2)

If yesterday we saw some examples of people who kept their faith in the face of denials of the fulfilment of God's promises, today we read of those who held to faith in the face of danger and persecution. There are some horrific stories that lie behind these brief and startling reports of flogging, stoning and other dreadful forms of torture. None more so, though, than the events of the end of Jesus' life to which this first week of Passiontide carries us.

That is why the writer to the Hebrews exhorts us – in the company of the 'cloud of witnesses' (12.1) – to look to Jesus, 'the pioneer and perfecter of our faith' (12.2). The exemplars of faith can inspire us, but only Jesus can save us. He not only shows us how to endure the trials and sufferings that come to God's people; he also blazes a trail through the suffering caused by the sin of the world and the chaos of the cosmos to find that joy in the presence of God for which humanity was created.

When our faith is tested in the face of danger and persecution, as it will undoubtedly be, we will need to look to Jesus both as the most excellent example of earthly faithfulness and as the heavenly Lord whose scars are the sign of God's victory over all the powers of evil.

Gracious Father,
you gave up your Son
out of love for the world:
lead us to ponder the mysteries of his passion,
that we may know eternal peace
through the shedding of our Saviour's blood,
Jesus Christ our Lord.

COLLECT

Wednesday 9 April

Hebrews 12.3-13

'...in order that we may share his holiness' (v.10)

Hebrews has been struggling to resolve a dilemma. How can human beings, with all their failings, enter into the pure and holy presence of God? The answer at which it arrives is that 'we have been sanctified through the offering of the body of Jesus Christ once for all' (Hebrews 10.10).

In the words of chapter 11's great refrain, it is 'by faith' that we receive the gift of sanctified status as we trust that, in the words of the eucharistic prayer, God 'has counted us worthy to stand in his presence and serve him'. At the same time, as we step into the presence of God through faith, clothed in the gift of righteousness, we are called to live out that faith in an obedient life that leads to the 'peaceful fruit of righteousness' (v.11) growing within us and seen through us.

That is where the discipline of which the writer talks comes in. It is not, though, some form of punishment that is being described. Rather, it is the shaping process that comes through facing and bearing the inevitable cost of following the one whom the world rejected. As we meet the challenges of Christian living with obedience, so the character of Jesus begins to form within us.

Faith and obedience, though different, are not opposed because, as Dietrich Bonhoeffer writes in *The Cost of Discipleship*: 'Only the believers obey, and only the obedient believe.'

COLLECT

Most merciful God,
who by the death and resurrection of your Son Jesus Christ
delivered and saved the world:
grant that by faith in him who suffered on the cross
we may triumph in the power of his victory;
through Jesus Christ your Son our Lord,
who is alive and reigns with you,
in the unity of the Holy Spirit,
one God, now and for ever.

Psalms **40**, 125 *or* 56, **57** (63*)
Exodus 9.13-end
Hebrews 12.14-end

Hebrews 12.14-end

'See to it that no one fails to obtain the grace of God' (v.15)

Yesterday we thought about how we are led by the crucified hand of Jesus Christ into the presence of God. Today we see something of the awesome scene around the consuming fire of God's presence. The 'innumerable angels', the 'assembly of the firstborn' and the 'spirits of the righteous' surround God, who is 'judge of all' (vv.22-23). No wonder Moses said 'I tremble with fear' (v.21) even before the earthly mountain, the pale shadow of the heavenly city. Fear though, for us, is cast out by the perfect love of God in the gift of his Son, 'Jesus, the mediator of a new covenant' (v.24).

The pure gift of the grace of God in Christ, proved in the privileges of Christian worship, is also to be practised in the relationships of life. 'Pursue peace with everyone' (v.14), implores the writer. Do not let bitterness take root. Otherwise you will find yourselves, perhaps as unaware as Esau, selling your birthright, disinheriting the blessing and failing to obtain the grace of God (v.15).

What could be a greater tragedy than missing out on the grace of God? Perhaps we could make this our motivation for the Holy Week that lies ahead of us: that we will not allow ourselves or our families, our friends or our colleagues, our communities or our churches to fail to receive the grace of God, the grace that consumes us with the fire of divine love.

Gracious Father,
you gave up your Son
out of love for the world:
lead us to ponder the mysteries of his passion,
that we may know eternal peace
through the shedding of our Saviour's blood,
Jesus Christ our Lord.

COLLECT

Psalms **22**, 126 *or* **51**, 54
Exodus 10
Hebrews 13.1-16

Hebrews 13.1-16

'Remember those who are in prison, as though you were in prison with them' (v.3)

It is the sort of thing we say as Christians – 'let mutual love continue' (v.1). But the writer takes us very deep into the sort of love that we are to practise and the extent of the mutuality that membership of the body of Christ entails.

The Church to which the letter is written is in a very hostile environment, with many believers imprisoned and some being tortured. Remember those who are *bound* as though you were *bound* with them, implores the writer, playing on the Greek word for prisoners. This is the sort of costly identification with those who are suffering for which the gospel calls, a practical empathy that could in the ancient world, as it can in some places today, involve a literal sharing in the actual conditions of detention.

Lest this sound too demanding, even unreasonable, the writer reminds us that it is 'well for the heart to be strengthened by grace' (v.9). The grace of our Lord Jesus Christ, the grace of the cross was well put by the second century bishop, Melito of Sardis, when he said that 'the Lord who had clothed himself with humanity was bound for the sake of the imprisoned'. For our liberation, Christ bound himself to us in the imprisonment of our sin and in the captivity of all that oppresses us. And so – in the words of the hymn – we sing: 'My chains fell off, my heart was free, I rose, went forth, and followed Thee'.

COLLECT

Most merciful God,
who by the death and resurrection of your Son Jesus Christ
delivered and saved the world:
grant that by faith in him who suffered on the cross
we may triumph in the power of his victory;
through Jesus Christ your Son our Lord,
who is alive and reigns with you,
in the unity of the Holy Spirit,
one God, now and for ever.

Psalms **23**, 127 *or* **68**
Exodus 11
Hebrews 13.17-end

Hebrews 13.17-end

'May the God of peace … make you complete in everything good'
(vv.20–21)

On the eve of Palm Sunday, as we prepare to enter Jerusalem with Jesus and relive the cruel events that led to his death, it is good to be reminded that all our commemorations take place in the light of the resurrection. It is heartening as well to have a hint of the great Easter blessing that will resound through our churches on the celebration of the Day of Resurrection, a blessing that follows the wording of verse 20 almost exactly.

At the heart of that blessing is that God will complete in us 'everything good' so that we will live in a way that is 'pleasing in his sight'. That is an extraordinarily bold vision of humanity. Through the power of the resurrection, human life is raised to the full stature of its dignity. We become not only objects and recipients of God's immeasurable grace and mercy but also subjects in the exercise of God's will and givers to God of the infinite joy of divine pleasure.

The glorious reality of Christian faith is that the new, redeemed humanity forged in the life, death and resurrection of Jesus Christ, given to us in word and sacrament, and received by us through faith, is to be lived out in Spirit-empowered, Christ-like lives that are – like Jesus' own life – pleasing in God's sight.

Gracious Father,
you gave up your Son
out of love for the world:
lead us to ponder the mysteries of his passion,
that we may know eternal peace
through the shedding of our Saviour's blood,
Jesus Christ our Lord.

COLLECT

Monday 14 April

Monday of Holy Week

Luke 22.1-23

'So he consented...' (v.6)

Last week we were inspired by some holy lives and holy living. This week we are confronted by a very unholy life and a set of most ungodly decisions. We do not see a life that is being raised to the full stature of human dignity but a person disintegrating before our eyes and being reduced, one choice at time, to a frightening level of inhumanity.

Yes, Judas was caught up in a cosmic conflict of evil against good. Yes, he found himself embroiled in the political manoeuvering of anxious national leaders. Yes, he was even a player in the providential plan in which 'the Son of Man is going as it has been determined' (v.22). Nevertheless, he was not an unwitting pawn. It can still be said of Judas that 'he consented'.

It takes two to tango. It takes an alignment between external pressure and internal permission to become entangled in the briars of sin and to sink into the sand of corruption. That is what is happening to Judas and that is his state of mind and heart as he sits at table with Jesus to share in the supper that, because of Judas' sin, will become Jesus' last.

'Let anyone among you who is without sin be the first to throw a stone' (John 8.7). I am no better than Judas. My consent, my sin, my betrayal would have been enough to send Jesus to his cross. Lord, have mercy.

COLLECT

Almighty and everlasting God,
who in your tender love towards the human race
    sent your Son our Saviour Jesus Christ
to take upon him our flesh
and to suffer death upon the cross:
grant that we may follow the example of his patience and humility,
and also be made partakers of his resurrection;
through Jesus Christ your Son our Lord,
who is alive and reigns with you,
in the unity of the Holy Spirit,
one God, now and for ever.

Psalm 27
Lamentations 3.1-18
Luke 22.[24-38] 39-53

Luke 22.[24-38] 39-53

'Judas ... approached Jesus to kiss him' (v.47)

'Is it with a kiss that you are betraying the Son of Man?' asks Jesus of his 'familiar friend', even his 'bosom friend' in whom he trusted, who ate of his bread (Psalm 55.13; 41.9).

Judas' arrogant, calculating, deceitful attempt of a kiss on the face of Jesus could not be a greater contrast with the impulsive overflow of affection of the woman whose tears bathed the feet of Jesus and whose kisses adored him. She too 'was a sinner' (Luke 7.37) but a sinner who was now keeling before the grace-filled presence of Jesus, 'ransomed, healed, restored, forgiven'.

There were other people in the room at the time. Simon, the Pharisee, was one of them. It was his house and he had invited Jesus to eat with him. When Simon began to question why Jesus, a would-be prophet, allowed *that woman* to act in this way, Jesus said to him, 'You gave me no kiss, but from the time I came in she has not stopped kissing my feet' (Luke 7.45).

The grace of the cross brings us to the point of decision. We are not afforded the luxury of Simon, holding back and observing. The choice is to turn away and betray, like Judas, or to turn towards and follow, like Mary the mother of our Saviour who, in Christina Rossetti's unforgettable words, 'worshipped the beloved with a kiss' at his birth and stood by the cross at his death.

True and humble king,
hailed by the crowd as Messiah:
grant us the faith to know you and love you,
that we may be found beside you
on the way of the cross,
which is the path of glory.

COLLECT

43

Wednesday 16 April

Wednesday of Holy Week

Psalm 102 [*or* 102.1-18]
Wisdom 1.16 – 2.1; 2.12–22
or Jeremiah 11.18-20
Luke 22.54-end

Luke 22.54-end

'The Lord turned and looked at Peter' (v.61)

What was it like to be looked at in that way at that moment? Peter had just denied that he was with Jesus, that he knew him and followed him. When Jesus first met Peter, so John tells us, he looked at Peter and saw in him strengths that even Peter had not dared to imagine. Jesus looked at him and knew him as he could be – not just Simon son of John, but *Cephas*, upon whose rock-like qualities Jesus would build his new community.

We do not know exactly how Jesus looked at Peter before the cock crowed. But we do know that 'Jesus Christ is the same yesterday, today and tomorrow'. His character is consistent, he can be relied upon to be faithful. So we can say confidently that Jesus would have looked at him and, even then, *loved him*, just as he had done with the rich young ruler whose spirit was willing but, like Peter, whose flesh was weak.

No wonder Peter 'went out and wept bitterly' (v.62), for to be looked at with that sort of love – the love that knows you and still believes in you even though you have condemned that love to death – was a hard and heavy burden to bear. But the kingdom Jesus promised, when he would eat and drink with his disciples again, was coming. And when it came, Peter said, 'Yes Lord, *you* know that I love you' (John 21.15-17).

COLLECT

Almighty and everlasting God,
who in your tender love towards the human race
    sent your Son our Saviour Jesus Christ
to take upon him our flesh
and to suffer death upon the cross:
grant that we may follow the example of his patience and humility,
and also be made partakers of his resurrection;
through Jesus Christ your Son our Lord,
who is alive and reigns with you,
in the unity of the Holy Spirit,
one God, now and for ever.

Psalms 42, 43
Leviticus 16.2-24
Luke 23.1-25

Luke 23.1-25

'[Pilate] released the one who had been put in prison for insurrection'
(v.25)

Last week we thought about the words of Melito of Sardis, that 'the Lord … was bound for the sake of the imprisoned'. Today we see that spiritual truth in historical reality. Jesus quite literally takes Barabbas' place. This is the substitution of the sinner by the sinless. This is Jesus being given over to the judgement that Barabbas deserved for 'insurrection and murder'.

We have all been involved in the insurrection against God's purposes. We have played our part in the murdering of the love that God has for the world. We have all set ourselves up at some point as enemies of God's state of peace and justice. But, though our 'voices' *against God* 'prevailed' before Pilate's seat, they are deafened by God's voice *for us* before the throne where the Lamb who has been slain is to be found.

'Love', as Austen Farrer, the twentieth-century Anglican philosopher, said, 'is the strongest instrument of omnipotence' and God uses this weapon of love with such a divine power that 'he bears our infirmities and carries our diseases' and is 'wounded for our transgressions, crushed for our iniquities' (Isaiah 53.4-5) in order – as Melito put it – 'to set the condemned free'.

As those who have been acquitted by the love of God, we are enlisted to contend with all that contends against God, armed only with, as the notable theologian and medical missionary Albert Schweitzer described it, 'the most powerful weapon you can use against your enemy' – love.

God our Father,
you have invited us to share in the supper
which your Son gave to his Church
to proclaim his death until he comes:
may he nourish us by his presence,
and unite us in his love;
who is alive and reigns with you,
in the unity of the Holy Spirit,
one God, now and for ever.

COLLECT

Friday 18 April

Good Friday

Psalm 69
Genesis 22.1-18
John 19.38-end
or Hebrews 10.1-10

Hebrews 10.1-10

'See, I have come to do your will' (v.9)

God's will is for human beings to reach their full dignity as creatures made in the image and likeness of God. God's will for humanity is to live the pattern of divinity in the sphere of creation. It is God's will to shape our species into a form of life that reflects God's joy and justice, peace and kindness, beauty and truth.

God wills a human life that offers itself obediently to God for God's good purposes. This is the will to which Jesus says 'yes' as he gives himself over to the cross. It is the same 'yes' that he said to the Father's will to send him in love to the world. It is the same 'yes' that he said in every step of his ministry as he gave himself in healing and hope, word and promise, praying each moment:

'Ready for all thy perfect will
My acts of faith and love repeat,
Till death thy endless mercies seal
And make my sacrifice complete.'

(Charles Wesley, 'O thou who camest from above')

Jesus says 'yes' to God's will for a holy humanity. This is the will that Jesus wills. This is the will that Jesus enacts as he offers his body once for all, for love of all. As he does so, the need for any other sacrifice of atonement falls away. For now a human being has been found who is *at one* with God. May we be found in him.

COLLECT

Almighty Father,
look with mercy on this your family
for which our Lord Jesus Christ was content to be betrayed
    and given up into the hands of sinners
    and to suffer death upon the cross;
who is alive and glorified with you and the Holy Spirit,
one God, now and for ever.

Psalm 142
Hosea 6.1-6
John 2.18-22

John 2.18-22

'But he was speaking of the temple of his body' (v.21)

Jesus' body had been destroyed on Friday, Good Friday. It had been racked by intolerable pain, ruined by slow starvation of oxygen and desecrated by penetration of nails and spear.

On Saturday, Holy Saturday, Jesus' body, destroyed by such an ugly death, lay limp on the cold stone of the dark tomb while his spirit descended to the region of the dead, even there proclaiming the gospel (1 Peter 4.6).

On Sunday, Easter Day, the Day of Resurrection, the prophecy would be fulfilled. The body of Jesus would be raised from the dead and the new, glorious temple of Christ's risen body would beckon all of humanity to step through the open doors of Jesus' wide embrace into the Holy of Holies of God's gracious presence.

So, believe the scripture and the word that Jesus spoke (v.22), and 'come to him, a living stone, though rejected by mortals yet chosen and precious in God's sight, and like living stones, let yourselves be built into a spiritual house, to be a holy priesthood, to offer spiritual sacrifices acceptable to God through Jesus Christ' (1 Peter 2.4-5).

COLLECT

Grant, Lord,
that we who are baptized into the death
of your Son our Saviour Jesus Christ
may continually put to death our evil desires
and be buried with him;
and that through the grave and gate of death
we may pass to our joyful resurrection;
through his merits,
who died and was buried and rose again for us,
your Son Jesus Christ our Lord.

Morning Prayer – a simple form

Preparation

O Lord, open our lips
and our mouth shall proclaim your praise.

A prayer of thanksgiving for Lent *(for Passiontide see p. 50)*

Blessed are you, Lord God of our salvation,
to you be glory and praise for ever.
In the darkness of our sin you have shone in our hearts
to give the light of the knowledge of the glory of God
in the face of Jesus Christ.
Open our eyes to acknowledge your presence,
that freed from the misery of sin and shame
we may grow into your likeness from glory to glory.
Blessed be God, Father, Son and Holy Spirit.
Blessed be God for ever.

Word of God

Psalmody *(the psalm or psalms listed for the day)*

Glory to the Father and to the Son
and to the Holy Spirit;
as it was in the beginning is now:
and shall be for ever. Amen.

Reading from Holy Scripture *(one or both of the passages set for the day)*

Reflection

The Benedictus (The Song of Zechariah) *(see opposite page)*

Prayers

Intercessions – a time of prayer for the day and its tasks, the world and its need, the church and her life.

The Collect for the Day

The Lord's Prayer *(see p. 51)*

Conclusion

A blessing or the Grace *(see p. 51)*, or a concluding response

Let us bless the Lord
Thanks be to God

Benedictus (The Song of Zechariah)

1   Blessed be the Lord the God of Israel, ◆
    who has come to his people and set them free.

2   He has raised up for us a mighty Saviour, ◆
    born of the house of his servant David.

3   Through his holy prophets God promised of old ◆
    to save us from our enemies,
        from the hands of all that hate us,

4   To show mercy to our ancestors, ◆
    and to remember his holy covenant.

5   This was the oath God swore to our father Abraham: ◆
    to set us free from the hands of our enemies,

6   Free to worship him without fear, ◆
    holy and righteous in his sight
        all the days of our life.

7   And you, child, shall be called the prophet of the Most High, ◆
    for you will go before the Lord to prepare his way,

8   To give his people knowledge of salvation ◆
    by the forgiveness of all their sins.

9   In the tender compassion of our God ◆
    the dawn from on high shall break upon us,

10 To shine on those who dwell in darkness
        and the shadow of death, ◆
    and to guide our feet into the way of peace.

Luke 1.68-79

**Glory to the Father and to the Son
and to the Holy Spirit;
as it was in the beginning is now:
and shall be for ever. Amen.**

Seasonal Prayers of Thanksgiving

Passiontide

Blessed are you, Lord God of our salvation,
to you be praise and glory for ever.
As a man of sorrows and acquainted with grief
your only Son was lifted up
that he might draw the whole world to himself.
May we walk this day in the way of the cross
and always be ready to share its weight,
declaring your love for all the world.
Blessed be God, Father, Son and Holy Spirit.
Blessed be God for ever.

At Any Time

Blessed are you, creator of all,
to you be praise and glory for ever.
As your dawn renews the face of the earth
bringing light and life to all creation,
may we rejoice in this day you have made;
as we wake refreshed from the depths of sleep,
open our eyes to behold your presence
and strengthen our hands to do your will,
that the world may rejoice and give you praise.
Blessed be God, Father, Son and Holy Spirit.
Blessed be God for ever.

after Lancelot Andrewes (1626)

The Lord's Prayer and The Grace

Our Father in heaven,
hallowed be your name,
your kingdom come,
your will be done,
on earth as in heaven.
Give us today our daily bread.
Forgive us our sins
as we forgive those who sin against us.
Lead us not into temptation
but deliver us from evil.
For the kingdom, the power,
and the glory are yours
now and for ever.
Amen.

(or)

Our Father, who art in heaven,
hallowed be thy name;
thy kingdom come;
thy will be done;
on earth as it is in heaven.
Give us this day our daily bread.
And forgive us our trespasses,
as we forgive those who trespass against us.
And lead us not into temptation;
but deliver us from evil.
For thine is the kingdom,
the power and the glory,
for ever and ever.
Amen.

The grace of our Lord Jesus Christ,
and the love of God,
and the fellowship of the Holy Spirit,
be with us all evermore.
Amen.

An Order for Night Prayer (Compline)

The Lord almighty grant us a quiet night and a perfect end.
Amen.

Our help is in the name of the Lord
who made heaven and earth.

A period of silence for reflection on the past day may follow.

The following or other suitable words of penitence may be used

**Most merciful God,
we confess to you,
before the whole company of heaven and one another,
that we have sinned in thought, word and deed
and in what we have failed to do.
Forgive us our sins,
heal us by your Spirit
and raise us to new life in Christ. Amen.**

O God, make speed to save us.
O Lord, make haste to help us.

**Glory to the Father and to the Son
and to the Holy Spirit;
as it was in the beginning is now
and shall be for ever. Amen.
Alleluia.**

The following or another suitable hymn may be sung

Before the ending of the day,
Creator of the world, we pray
That you, with steadfast love, would keep
Your watch around us while we sleep.

From evil dreams defend our sight,
From fears and terrors of the night;
Tread underfoot our deadly foe
That we no sinful thought may know.

O Father, that we ask be done
Through Jesus Christ, your only Son;
And Holy Spirit, by whose breath
Our souls are raised to life from death.

The Word of God

Psalmody

One or more of Psalms 4, 91 or 134 may be used.

Psalm 134

1   Come, bless the Lord, all you servants of the Lord, ◆
    you that by night stand in the house of the Lord.

2   Lift up your hands towards the sanctuary ◆
    and bless the Lord.

3   The Lord who made heaven and earth ◆
    give you blessing out of Zion.

**Glory to the Father and to the Son
and to the Holy Spirit;
as it was in the beginning is now
and shall be for ever. Amen.**

Scripture Reading

*One of the following short lessons or another suitable
passage is read*

You, O Lord, are in the midst of us and we are called by
your name; leave us not, O Lord our God.

Jeremiah 14.9

(or)

Be sober, be vigilant, because your adversary the devil is
prowling round like a roaring lion, seeking for someone
to devour. Resist him, strong in the faith.

1 Peter 5.8,9

(or)

The servants of the Lamb shall see the face of God, whose
name will be on their foreheads. There will be no more night:
they will not need the light of a lamp or the light of the sun,
for God will be their light, and they will reign for ever and
ever.

Revelation 22.4,5

The following responsory may be said

Into your hands, O Lord, I commend my spirit.
Into your hands, O Lord, I commend my spirit.
For you have redeemed me, Lord God of truth.
I commend my spirit.
Glory to the Father and to the Son
and to the Holy Spirit.
Into your hands, O Lord, I commend my spirit.

Or, in Easter

Into your hands, O Lord, I commend my spirit.
Alleluia, alleluia.
Into your hands, O Lord, I commend my spirit.
Alleluia, alleluia.
For you have redeemed me, Lord God of truth.
Alleluia, alleluia.
Glory to the Father and to the Son
and to the Holy Spirit.
Into your hands, O Lord, I commend my spirit.
Alleluia, alleluia.

Keep me as the apple of your eye.
Hide me under the shadow of your wings.

Gospel Canticle

Nunc Dimittis (The Song of Simeon)

Save us, O Lord, while waking,
and guard us while sleeping,
that awake we may watch with Christ
and asleep may rest in peace.

1   Now, Lord, you let your servant go in peace:
your word has been fulfilled.

2   My own eyes have seen the salvation
which you have prepared in the sight of every people;

3   A light to reveal you to the nations
and the glory of your people Israel.

Luke 2.29-32

Glory to the Father and to the Son
and to the Holy Spirit;
as it was in the beginning is now
and shall be for ever. Amen.

Save us, O Lord, while waking,
and guard us while sleeping,
that awake we may watch with Christ
and asleep may rest in peace.

Prayers

Intercessions and thanksgivings may be offered here.

The Collect

Visit this place, O Lord, we pray,
and drive far from it the snares of the enemy;
may your holy angels dwell with us and guard us in peace,
and may your blessing be always upon us;
through Jesus Christ our Lord.
Amen.

The Lord's Prayer (see p. 51) may be said.

The Conclusion

In peace we will lie down and sleep;
for you alone, Lord, make us dwell in safety.

Abide with us, Lord Jesus,
for the night is at hand and the day is now past.

As the night watch looks for the morning,
so do we look for you, O Christ.

[Come with the dawning of the day
and make yourself known in the breaking of the bread.]

The Lord bless us and watch over us;
the Lord make his face shine upon us and be gracious to us;
the Lord look kindly on us and give us peace.
Amen.

Love what you've read?

Why not consider using *Reflections for Daily Prayer* all year round? We also publish these Bible notes in an annual format, containing material for the entire church year.

The volume for the 2014/15 church year will be published in May 2014 and features contributions from a host of distinguished writers: Gillian Cooper, Peter Graystone, Joanne Grenfell, Malcolm Guite, Lincoln Harvey, Mark Ireland, Rosalyn Murphy, Martyn Percy, John Pritchard, Ben Quash, Angela Tilby, Frances Ward, Lucy Winkett and Jeremy Worthen.

Reflections for Daily Prayer:
Advent 2014 to the eve of Advent 2015

ISBN 978 0 7151 4366 7
£16.99
Available May 2014

Can't wait for next year?

You can still pick up this year's edition of *Reflections*, direct from us (see details opposite for how to order) or from your local Christian bookshop.

Reflections for Daily Prayer:
Advent 2013 to the eve of Advent 2014

ISBN 978 0 7151 4362 9
£16.99 • Available Now

Reflections for Daily Prayer
App

Make Bible study and reflection a part of your routine wherever you go with the Reflections for Daily Prayer App for iPhone, iPad and iPod Touch.

Download the app for free from the Apple App Store and receive a week's worth of reflections free.
Then purchase a monthly, three-monthly or annual subscription to receive up-to-date content.

Use your iPhone QR code reader to scan this symbol and visit the Reflections for Daily Prayer page at the App store.

Orders can be made at **www.chpublishing.co.uk**
or via **Norwich Books and Music**
Telephone **(01603) 785923**
E-mail **orders@norwichbooksandmusic.co.uk**

Resources for Daily Prayer

Common Worship: Daily Prayer

The official daily office of the Church of England,
Common Worship: Daily Prayer is a rich collection of
devotional material that will enable those wanting to enrich
their quiet times to develop a regular pattern of prayer.

It includes:

- Prayer During the Day
- Forms of Penitence
- Morning and Evening Prayer
- Night Prayer (Compline)
- Collects and Refrains
- Canticles
- Complete Psalter

896 pages • with 6 ribbons • 202 x 125mm

Hardback	978 0 7151 2199 3	**£22.50**
Soft cased	978 0 7151 2178 8	**£27.50**
Bonded leather	978 0 7151 2100 9	**£45.00**